STEM trailblazer BIOS

SPACEX AND TESLA MOTORS ENGINEER
ELON MUSK

MATT DOEDEN

Lerner Publications
Minneapolis

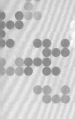

Lerner Publications Company
A division of Lerner Publishing Group, Inc.
241 First Avenue North
Minneapolis, MN 55401 USA

For reading levels and more information, look up this title at www.lernerbooks.com.

Content Consultant: John Weyrauch, Industrial Professor of Design, Aerospace Engineering and Mechanics, University of Minnesota

Library of Congress Cataloging-in-Publication Data

Doeden, Matt.
    SpaceX and Tesla Motors engineer Elon Musk / by Matt Doeden.
        pages   cm. — (STEM trailblazer bios)
    Includes bibliographical references and index.
    ISBN 978-1-4677-5791-1 (lib. bdg. : alk. paper)
    ISBN 978-1-4677-6280-9 (eBook)
    1. Musk, Elon. 2. Businesspeople—United States—Biography—Juvenile literature.
3. Businesspeople—South Africa—Biography—Juvenile literature. 4. Internet industry—Juvenile
literature. 5. PayPal (Firm)—Juvenile literature. 6. Clean energy industries—Juvenile literature.
7. SpaceX (Firm)—Juvenile literature. 8. Tesla Motors—Juvenile literature. I. Title.
HC102.5.M88D64 2015
338.7'6292293092—dc23 [B]   2014018979

Manufactured in the United States of America
1 – PC – 12/31/14

The images in this book are used with the permission of: Courtesy of NASA, p. 4; © SpaceX,
pp. 5, 22, 23; © iStockphoto.com/ManoAfrica, p. 6; © Alexander Joe/AFP/Getty Images, p. 7;
© iStockphoto.com/xxz114, p. 9; © Daniel Acker/Bloomberg/Getty Images, pp. 10, 24; © Patrick T.
Fallon/Bloomberg/Getty Images, p. 11; AP Photo/Paul Sakuma, pp. 13, 17; Paul Harris/BWP Media/
Newscom, p. 14; CB2/ZOB/WENN/Newscom, p. 15; © Car Culture/CORBIS, p. 18; © Axel Koester/
CORBIS, p. 20; © AF Archive/Alamy, p. 21; AP Photo/Tesla Motors, p. 25; © John B. Carnett/
Popular Science via Getty Images, p. 27.

Front cover: © AFP Photo/ANP/Jerry Lampen/Getty Images.

Main body text set in Adrianna Regular 13/22. Typeface provided by Chank.

CONTENTS

The Dragon cargo spacecraft soars in orbit above Earth. Elon Musk's company SpaceX built the Dragon.

FROM SOUTH AFRICA TO SILICON VALLEY

Elon Musk has always set his goals high. As a kid, he dreamed of becoming an astronaut and traveling to Mars. He loved to read science fiction stories. These tales of wild futures and imaginary technology filled him with excitement about what people might one day achieve.

Born June 28, 1971, in Pretoria, South Africa, Musk was curious about everything. When he wasn't reading, he was exploring. But by the time he was ten, his biggest love was technology. Personal computers were still fairly new. So were video games. Musk wanted to create his own games. So he saved up his allowance and bought a computer. Then he started teaching himself to write computer programs.

He was a quick study. At the age of twelve, Musk created a game called *Blast Star.* And he sold the game's **code** to a computer magazine! Already, he had a knack for combining tech smarts with business sense.

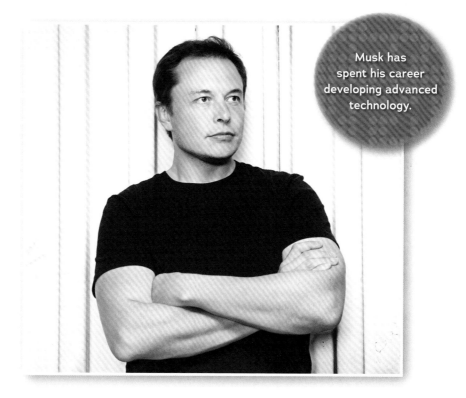

Musk has spent his career developing advanced technology.

Musk grew up in Pretoria, South Africa.

LEAVING HOME

In high school, Musk was the youngest and smallest boy in his class. He was often bullied. Musk found comfort in books and computers. But it was a very lonely time in his life.

It was also a difficult time in the history of South Africa. The nation was ruled by a racist political party. A policy called **apartheid** officially separated black people and white people. This was a way of keeping South Africa's white **minority** in power. Black and mixed-race people had fewer rights.

Musk didn't agree with apartheid. But as a white male, he was expected to support the government. All white men had to serve in South Africa's military for a few years. Musk knew that once he finished high school, he'd have to join the military. That meant enforcing the government's racist policies.

So Musk made a big decision. After high school, he would leave South Africa. His parents didn't like this plan. But Musk was determined to make a new life for himself. The seventeen-year-old traveled halfway across the world to Canada.

Nelson Mandela *(center)* fought against apartheid in South Africa. He became the country's first black president in 1994.

COLLEGE BOUND

Musk enrolled at Queen's School of Business in Kingston, Ontario. (Kimbal, his younger brother, later joined him there.) He had very little money. Often he struggled just to afford a meal. But that changed in 1992 when he earned a **scholarship** to the Wharton School of Business at the University of Pennsylvania.

Musk earned a degree in economics. He was excited about getting out into the real world. He wanted to make his mark. But he wasn't yet sure how he would do that. He had three main interests. The first was space travel, his childhood passion. The second was **clean energy**—energy that doesn't damage the environment. The third was the Internet, which was just starting to become widely used. Which passion would he pursue?

TECH TALK

"A lot of times the question is harder than the answer. If you can properly phrase the question, then the answer is the easy part. [The better we] understand the universe, then [the better] we can . . . know what questions to ask."

—Elon Musk

Silicon Valley is home to many tech companies. The area is located near San Francisco, California.

Hoping to answer that question, Musk turned his studies to **physics**. In 1995, he was accepted to graduate school at Stanford University. So he headed to California. It was the perfect place for him to be. Stanford is in the area of California called Silicon Valley—the heart of the tech world. There, Musk saw young people doing exactly what he wanted to do—starting tech businesses that could create big changes. He couldn't wait any longer. "I could either watch it happen or be a part of it," he later wrote. So after just two days at Stanford, he dropped out.

Chapter 2

Musk has worked hard to establish companies that improve technology.

BUILDING AN EMPIRE

Musk didn't just quit school without a plan. He'd spotted an opportunity. In the mid-1990s, newspapers around the world were beginning to focus on their websites. But websites were expensive to maintain. The newspapers needed a way to make money off their sites. So in 1995, Musk and his brother, Kimbal, started a company called Zip2. Their plan was to provide newspapers with city guides. These guides would directly connect newspapers' websites to local businesses. Then the businesses could pay the newspapers to advertise on the papers' websites. It was a win for everyone involved.

Musk threw himself into his work. It was a struggle at first. Money was tight. Musk slept in his office. He showered at a nearby YMCA. But he didn't mind. He wasn't trying to get rich. He just wanted a chance to pursue his passions. "I didn't really expect to make any money," he said later. "If I could make enough to cover the rent and buy some food, that would be fine."

Musk started his first company with his younger brother, Kimbal (right).

Musk stuck with it, and his idea proved to be a winner. Soon, Zip2 was **licensing** its software to newspapers such as the *New York Times* and the *Chicago Tribune*. Profits were rolling in. In 1999, Musk and his **investors** sold Zip2 to the Compaq computer company. Compaq paid more than $300 million! Just like that, Musk was a multimillionaire.

PAYPAL

Musk wasn't the only young tech whiz getting rich during the late 1990s. Technology was booming, especially the Internet. **Dot-com** millionaires seemed to be everywhere. Many of them were one-hit wonders. Musk, on the other hand, had more ideas up his sleeve.

TECH TALK

"If you go back a few hundred years, what we take for granted today would seem like magic—being able to talk to people over long distances, to transmit images, flying. . . . So engineering is, for all intents and purposes, magic. And who wouldn't want to be a magician?"

—*Elon Musk*

PayPal chief executive officer Peter Thiel *(left)* poses for a photo with Musk in October 2000.

Musk noticed that as the Internet grew more popular, more people were making payments online. But there was no safe, reliable way to do this. Banks were slow to fill the need. So in 1999, Musk started an online bank, X.com. Through his bank, customers could send and receive payments by e-mail.

Others had the same idea, including rival company PayPal. Through X.com, Musk bought PayPal in 2000. He combined it with his own service, keeping the PayPal name. In 2001, he sold PayPal to online auction site eBay for a jaw-dropping $1.5 billion.

Everything seemed to be going well for Musk. He had recently married his longtime girlfriend, Justine Wilson. He was extremely wealthy. The only question was what he would do next.

Chapter 3

Musk reviews an artist's impression of a SpaceX rocket in March 2004.

CHASING DREAMS

In the summer of 2002, Musk thought back to his childhood dream. He'd always wanted to be an astronaut. But he was disappointed with the US space program. Manned spaceflight had been on the decline. NASA was using old technology. Nobody seemed interested in new advancements. If he ever wanted to go to space, he'd need to build his own spaceship.

SPACEX

Musk couldn't achieve his mission alone. So he introduced himself to engineer Tom Mueller. Mueller shared Musk's passion for spaceflight. In his garage, Mueller was building his own rocket. Musk made Mueller an offer he couldn't refuse—the chance to lead a new company dedicated to reaching for the stars.

SpaceX planned for its rockets to be reusable. This would make rockets cheaper to operate and better for the environment.

In June 2002, Musk started Space Exploration Technologies (SpaceX). The company's goal was to build reusable rockets. Musk put Mueller in charge of rocket design. SpaceX was already testing new rockets by 2003.

SpaceX's first priority is to cheaply get people and cargo into space. But Musk also has a long-term plan. He wants SpaceX to lead the charge in private space exploration. He hopes to send humans to Mars by the mid-2020s. Eventually, he wants to start a permanent human settlement there.

To some, this may sound unrealistic. But Musk believes it's natural for humans to explore and settle new territories. If his dreams become reality, he says he'll retire on Mars. Meanwhile, he's working to transform the planet he currently calls home.

TECH TALK

"I like to be involved in things that change the world. The Internet did, and space will probably be more responsible for changing the world than anything else. If humanity can expand beyond the Earth, obviously that's where the future is."

—Elon Musk

Tesla workers assemble an electric car at the company's showroom in September 2008.

ELECTRIFYING THE AUTO MARKET

In 2004, Musk helped start another new company, Tesla Motors. Tesla's goal is to produce entirely electric cars. Musk has always cared deeply about clean energy. He loved the idea of making cars that didn't rely on gasoline.

Few people thought Tesla had a chance at success. Small car companies had trouble competing with bigger names. And clean energy cars were underdogs against traditional gas-powered vehicles. Even Musk didn't expect Tesla to survive for long. But he strongly believed in the company's mission.

Musk helped design the company's first **model**, the Tesla Roadster. This sleek sports car was released in 2006. It ran on a giant rechargeable battery instead of gas. Drivers could charge the car's battery at a charging station. Then they could go more than 200 miles (322 kilometers) without recharging. The Roadster was a huge hit. But its price tag—more than $100,000—made it too expensive for most drivers.

The Tesla Roadster uses a giant battery to run the engine.

TECH TALK

"In short, the master plan is:

1. Build [a] sports car.

2. Use that money to build an affordable car.

3. Use *that* money to build an even more affordable car.

. . . Don't tell anyone."

—*Elon Musk*

Musk knew that the Roadster was just a first step. He planned to make each future Tesla model less expensive than the one before it. In 2008, Musk became Tesla's chief executive officer. As CEO, he is officially in charge of managing the company. Eventually, he vowed, he would bring the price of a Tesla car down to $30,000—or lower!

Chapter 4

Musk *(front)* watches as the Falcon 1 rocket attempts to lift off in 2008.

NEW VISIONS

Despite all his successes, Musk was going through some rough times. By 2008, SpaceX had tried three test launches. All three had failed. The company was losing millions. Tesla was losing money too. Musk had sunk all he had into these companies. If they failed, his business empire could be shattered forever.

That same year, Musk and his wife, Justine, decided to divorce. All in all, 2008 was not going well for Musk. He later called it the worst year of his life.

Yet in tech circles, he was more of a legend than ever. In the 2008 film *Iron Man*, billionaire Tony Stark uses advanced technology to fight evil. Many fans noticed similarities between the film's hero and Musk. And director Jon Favreau later admitted that the character was partly based on the real-life billionaire. Musk even appeared in *Iron Man 2* two years later!

Robert Downey Jr. plays the wealthy businessman Tony Stark in the *Iron Man* movies.

BIG PLANS

Musk may not have been battling villains in an iron suit. But he was still chasing big dreams. And as quickly as his life had fallen apart, the pieces started falling back into place.

In September 2008, SpaceX tried a fourth test launch. This time, it was a success! The company's Falcon 1 rocket became the first privately built rocket ever to enter Earth's orbit. That same year, SpaceX scored a multibillion-dollar deal with NASA. Musk's rockets would carry cargo to and from the International Space Station.

The Falcon 9 was the second rocket developed by the SpaceX team. It first launched in 2010.

The Dragon v2 was designed to carry people into orbit. The vehicle was built in partnership with NASA.

Musk wasted no time. By 2012, a new spacecraft, the Dragon, was ready for action. It brought food, water, and clothing to the space station—then returned to Earth. And that was just the beginning. Next up was the Dragon v2 in 2014. This craft transports people instead of cargo. It can carry up to seven passengers. According to Musk, the age of the "space taxi" was around the corner.

Musk unveils the Model S electric car at an auto show in Detroit, Michigan.

Meanwhile, Tesla was becoming a growing force in the auto world. Under Musk's leadership, sales rose. The company stopped losing money. In 2012, Tesla's new car, the Model S, made headlines and broke sales records for electric cars.

Tesla also started building charging stations along highways. Drivers can stop at any charging station and recharge their cars' batteries for free. Musk was so proud of the "supercharger" network that he tried it himself. In 2014, he took his family on a road trip from Los Angeles, California, to New York City. He drove his Model S, which he recharged at superchargers along the way.

Musk still wasn't out of ideas, though. In 2013, he proposed building a new kind of transportation called the Hyperloop. The Hyperloop would be a sort of combination train and airplane. One-person pods would travel through a system of tubes. The pods would move at 800 miles (1,287 km) per hour, dragged along by very powerful magnets. Musk claimed the Hyperloop would allow for travel between the California cities of San Francisco and Los Angeles in just thirty minutes. That's faster than even a jet airplane can make the trip!

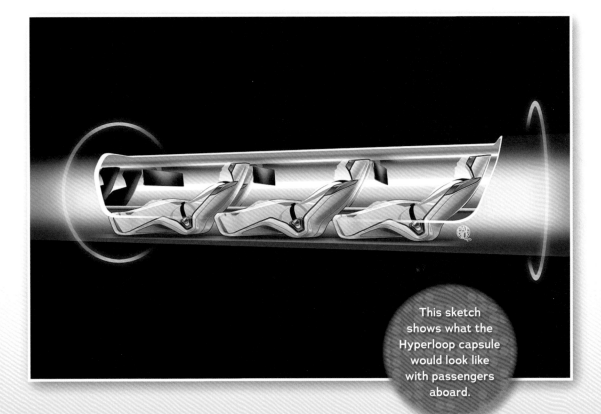

This sketch shows what the Hyperloop capsule would look like with passengers aboard.

THE FUTURE

People have often doubted Musk. Some said space travel was too complicated and expensive for private business. Others said that fully electric cars couldn't compete with gasoline-burning cars. Musk has proved his critics wrong time after time.

What more can Musk achieve? Will electric cars, led by Tesla, replace gas-fueled cars in the coming years? Can Musk really build a lasting community on another planet? It may sound like science fiction. But for Musk, almost anything seems possible.

TECH TALK

"If you imagine the future we want and say, 'that would be a good one,' . . . you'd want to have a future . . . where our species is out there exploring the stars. That would be great."

—Elon Musk

Musk's passion for clean energy is the driving force behind his work at Tesla.

TIMELINE

1971

Elon Musk is born on June 28 in Pretoria, South Africa.

1983

Musk creates and sells the code for a video game, *Blast Star*.

1989

Musk moves to Canada to attend Queen's School of Business.

1995

Musk begins classes at Stanford as a graduate student in physics but leaves school to start his own company, Zip2.

1999

Musk and his investors sell Zip2, earning him millions of dollars.

2002

Musk starts SpaceX with the goal of putting private rockets into space.

2004

Musk invests in and helps to run Tesla Motors, a company that builds fully electric cars.

2008

SpaceX has its first successful launch of the Falcon 1 rocket.

2013

Musk proposes a new transportation system called the Hyperloop that would allow travelers to go from Los Angeles to San Francisco in just thirty minutes.

2014

SpaceX introduces a "space taxi," the Dragon v2 spacecraft.

SOURCE NOTES

8 Alison van Diggelen, "Elon Musk: His Remarkable Story in His Own Words," *Fresh Dialogues*, January 29, 2013, http://www.freshdialogues .com/2013/01/29/elon-musk-his-remarkable-story-in-his-own-words -video.

9 Stephanie Lerner, *Kids Who Think Outside the Box: Helping Your Unique Child Thrive in a Cookie-Cutter World* (New York: AMACOM, 2005), 59.

11 Evan Carmichael, "The Wired Entrepreneur: The Early Years of Elon Musk," *Evan Carmichael*, May 22, 2014, http://www.evancarmichael .com/Famous-Entrepreneurs/1610/The-Wired-Entrepreneur-The-Early -Years-of-Elon-Musk.html.

12 Hannah Elliott, "At Home with Elon Musk: The (Soon-to-Be) Bachelor Billionaire," *Forbes*, March 26, 2012, http://www.forbes.com/sites /hannahelliott/2012/03/26/at-home-with-elon-musk-the-soon-to-be -bachelor-billionaire.

16 Josh Friedman, "Entrepreneur Tries His Midas Touch in Space," *Los Angeles Times*, April 22, 2003, http://articles.latimes.com/2003 /apr/22/business/fi-spacex22.

19 Elon Musk, "The Secret Tesla Motors Master Plan (Just Between You and Me)," *Tesla Motors*, August 2, 2006, http://www.teslamotors.com /blog/secret-tesla-motors-master-plan-just-between-you-and-me.

26 Nathan Gardels, "Innovations That Will Change Your Life: A Conversation with Elon Musk," *WorldPost*, January 21, 2014, http://www .huffingtonpost.com/2014/01/21/elon-musk-interview_n_4613227.html.

GLOSSARY

apartheid
a system of government-enforced racial segregation that existed in South Africa from 1948 until 1994

clean energy
sources of energy, such as solar and wind, that do not damage the environment

code
information in the form of letters, numbers, or symbols that can be read by a computer

dot-com
related to the Internet

investors
people or companies that put money into a company or a project in return for a share of the profits later

licensing
allowing a person or a company to use a product without owning it

minority
a group of people who are outnumbered by another group

model
a specific type or version of a product

physics
the study of matter and energy and how they interact

scholarship
money awarded to a student to help pay for schooling and living expenses

LERNER
SOURCE

Expand learning beyond the printed book. Download free, complementary educational resources for this book from our website, www.lernersource.com.

FURTHER
INFORMATION

BOOKS

Doeden, Matt. *Human Travel to the Moon and Mars: Waste of Money or Next Frontier?* Minneapolis: Twenty-First Century Books, 2012. What are the costs and possible payoffs of missions to Mars? Is human settlement on Mars possible? Find out what astronauts, politicians, and NASA officials think.

Green, Sara. *Elon Musk.* Minneapolis: Bellwether Media, 2014. Read more about the life and work of Elon Musk.

Hunter, Nick. *How Electric and Hybrid Cars Work.* New York: Gareth Stevens Publishing, 2014. Learn about the technology behind electric cars.

WEBSITES

How Electric Cars Work
http://auto.howstuffworks.com/electric-car.htm
Discover the ins and outs of electric cars and what makes them different from gasoline-burning vehicles.

SpaceX
http://www.spacex.com
Learn more about SpaceX, its rockets, space capsules, and much more at the company's official website.

Tesla Motors
http://www.teslamotors.com
Check out what Tesla Motors has to offer and how its electric cars work, and discover where you can see the cars in person.

INDEX

ABOUT THE AUTHOR

Matt Doeden studied journalism at Mankato State University, where he worked at the college newspaper for three years. Doeden went on to work as a sportswriter for the Mankato paper and then got a job as an editor for a children's book publisher. In 2003, Doeden decided to start his own business as a freelance writer and editor. Since then, he has written and edited hundreds of books on high-interest topics such as cars, sports, and airplanes, as well as curricular topics such as geography, science, and math.